18 HOLES TO RETIREMENT

A Diaglogue about a Well-Planned, Nearly Tax-Free Retirement

Al Smith

Golden Eagle Financial, Ltd.

Copyright © 2021 Golden Eagle Financial, Ltd.

All rights reserved

The characters and events portrayed in this book are fictitious. Any similarity to real persons, living or dead, is coincidental and not intended by the author.

No part of this book may be reproduced, or stored in a retrieval system, or transmitted in any form or by any means, electronic, mechanical, photocopying, recording, or otherwise, without express written permission of the publisher.

Printed in the United States of America

CONTENTS

Title Page
Copyright
Epigraph

Foreword
Eighteen Holes to Retirement					1
Acknowledgement						19
About The Author						21

This book is dedicated to Daniel Siedlecki, who loves golf and loves the Lord more.

"Golf is the closest game to the game we call life. You get bad breaks from good shots; you get good breaks from bad shots- but you have to play where it lies."

BOBBY JONES

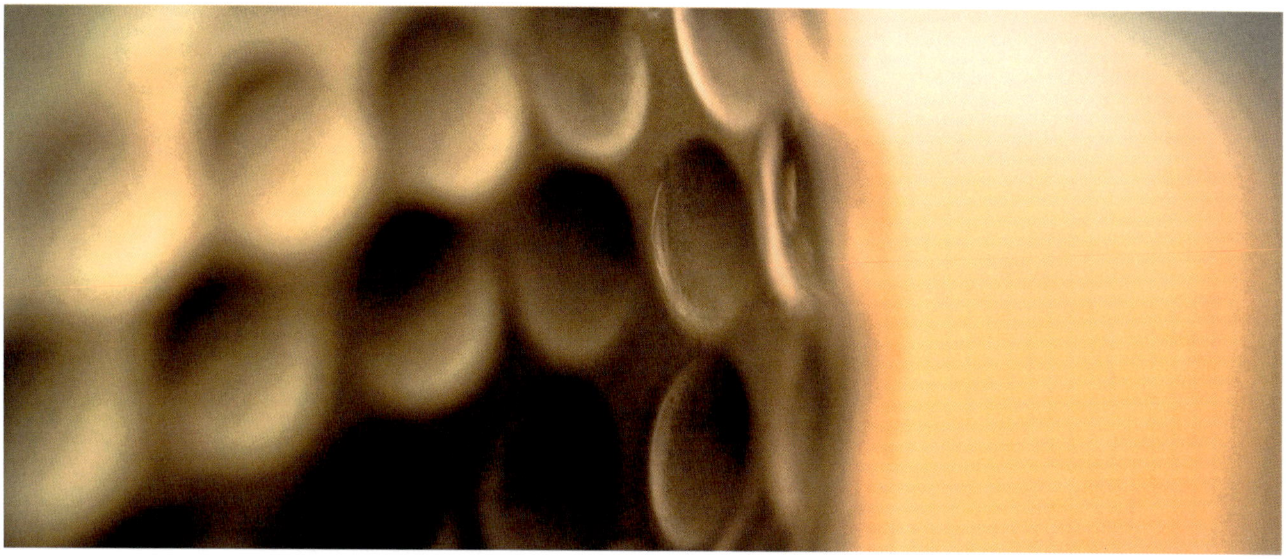

FOREWORD

This book shares a revealing conversation between two coworkers discussing retirement over a game of golf. This handy guide (or resource) is full of practical information that is easy to understand and applicable. It contains extremely valuable information for anyone near or in retirement. It uncovers information not typically discussed in order to educate and prepare one for the final stage of life.

It is my intention for the reader to gain the necessary knowledge to enter into life's last adventure with confidence and satisfaction...and without fear. Finding joy and fullfillment along the way.

-You do not have to like or play golf to enjoy this book!

EIGHTEEN HOLES TO RETIREMENT

A Dialogue about a Well-Planned, Nearly Tax-Free Retirement

"Alex, I knew I would find you at the putting green," Emmett said.

"You must also know that my short game needs a lot of work," Alex replied. "Have you checked in with the starter?" Alex asked.

"Yes, we're good to go. Let's get our cart and head out to the tee." Emmett responded.

The first hole was a par four with a reasonably wide fairway and some trees on the right. Alex hit first and achieved good distance but was near the trees on the right. Emmett's drive was a bit shorter but in the center of the fairway.

"So Emmett, are you and Jane excited about your upcoming retirement?" Alex asked.

"Absolutely Alex, we have been planning this for a long time."

Both took their second shots, neither reached the green but were close.

"You know Jane has worked for ABC Widget Company for 27 years....she is really looking forward to traveling and spending time with our grandkids." Emmett stated.

Both men chipped onto the green.....Emmett's shot left him about 18 feet away. Alex's rolled past the pin and down the slope leaving him a forty foot putt. After Emmett got his bogie and Alex three putted, they headed to number two tee.

"How can you be sure you will have enough money to live on in retirement?" Alex asked.

"Good question, considering you are a long way from retirement yourself." Emmett answered. " A few years ago we switched financial advisors. We now work with a fiduciary who specializes in retirement planning. Our old broker didn't do a poor job.....our assets grew but he never addressed our concerns about the taxation of our retirement benefits or how we could make certain that our money would last as long as we live."

Number two was also a par four with a dogleg to the left.....trees on the left and a creek about one hundred yards from the green made the hole difficult. Emmett hit a good drive slightly to the left but not in trouble. Alex sliced one off to the right....he was not in trouble but being off to the right made the hole a lot longer.

"So how did this new advisor provide you with the certainty that you and Jane will not run out of money?" Alex asked.

"Alex you know that my previous company provided me with a pension, right?" Emmett queried.

"Yes I remember you telling me that." Alex answered.

"Well when I reached 59 ½ I moved part of my current 401(k) into an indexed product that will provide a lifetime income for both Jane and me. The way it is structured, the lifetime income will increase in the years when there is positive growth, which it has been doing in the recent past. Its like my own personal pension." Emmett stated.

They each hit their second shots....Alex's landed just short of the creek about one hundred yards out. Emmett's was closer....about forty yards from the green on the left. They each took their third shots....Emmett's landed only ten feet from the pin....Alex's was about 24 feet away from the pin up a slight hill. Emmett made his putt for a par....Alex two putted.

"Both you and Jane will be collecting Social Security right?" Alex asked.

"Yes, but our plan is to postpone filing for benefits until age 70." Emmett stated.

"Why wouldn't you want to begin collecting sooner? Won't you both be missing out on all that income you would have received by filing earlier?" Alex asked.

"That's what we thought until our advisor did an analysis. We figured we needed $85,000 per year to live in retirement. Each of our Social Security benefits at full retirement age is about $2500 per month. By postponing filing Social Security till age 70 we will need to supplement our income with only $4,000 per year to meet our retirement objective. Based on that, all our Social Security is untaxed and our Federal Income tax is zero although we are living on an annual income of $85,000.

The third hole was a hundred and sixty yard par three with bunkers on each side of the green. Both men avoided the bunkers....Alex overshot a little and was on the fringe at the back.....Emmett's shot landed toward the front of the green on the right leaving him a long uphill putt. Alex made a really good chip and was able to one putt....Emmett two putted and each got their pars.

"Won't the income from your and Jane's 401(k)s and IRAs cause you to be in a higher tax bracket? I know you have both been saving for a very longtime." Alex asked.

"We were thinking the same thing until our advisor explained that if we convert part of our IRAs to Roth between now... we are both 61.... and age 72, the taxation on our remaining IRAs will be much less. Also once the Roth IRAs are 5 years old, all the income they generate is tax free." Emmett explained.

The fourth hole was a par five.....it curved slightly to the right. The green and pin could be seen only when you were halfway there. Emmett and Alex both hit good drives and their second shots left them only about one hundred yards out. Alex was in the rough on the right and Emmett was in the middle of the fairway as he often was. Both reached the green and two putted for their pars.

Number five was a par four with greater difficulty. Although not long, about 390 yards, a bunker presented a hazard on the left and water to the right of the fairway which, although wide, didn't seem that way if you didn't hit your drive straight. Alex sliced his drive into the water...Emmett's drive headed toward the bunker but was just short.

Alex took the penalty stroke....his second drive was slightly to the right but stayed out of the water. Both reached the green on their second shots and two putted.

Alex mentioned that his grandmother had been living in assisted living since his grandfather died a few years earlier. Emmett carried the conversation further when he mentioned that Jane's mother has been receiving care in her home for about two years.

"Isn't that really expensive?" Alex asked.

"Well it's not cheap, but her mom wanted to remain in her home which is on one level and is near us and Jane's sister. Her mom purchased a life insurance policy a number of years ago after Jane's dad died. The plan provides an advance of the death benefit if the insured person becomes chronically ill. It has been paying about half the cost of her care." Emmett explained.

"It sounds like you and your family have thought of everything." Alex exclaimed.

"Well our advisor describes 'Extended Care' as the Elephant in the room of Retirement Planning. Both Jane and I have similar plans that we started once we learned of her mom's situation. Because we started them when we were in our fifties, the benefit is quite healthy and the cost moderate, considering the high cost of care."

The sixth hole was a hundred and fifty yard par three with water on the left and trees on the right. Sand traps were on each side of the green which sits up high with a sharp drop off to the right. Alex's shot had the distance but was off to the right….missing the sand trap, but leaving him with a difficult approach. Emmett's shot landed on the front of the green. Fortunately the pin placement was also near the front of the green. Alex chipped up and was left with a twelve foot putt. Emmett missed his birdie putt…Alex two putted and they moved on to seven.

Seven was a longer par four….about 440 yards….with a dogleg to the left and slightly uphill. Alex's drive was farther but to the right in the rough. Emmett's landed near the center of the fairway leaving him a long but clear second shot. Both their second shots fell short of the green leaving them each a short approach. Emmett made an excellent approach shot leaving him with only a six foot putt. Alex's approach rolled to the back of the green from where he two putted. Emmett made his putt to save his par.

"What would you suggest for someone my age?" Alex asked.

"That's a good question." Emmett replied "Most of your peers, even those with healthy incomes, don't think that far ahead." Emmett stated.

Eight was a birdieable (is that even a word) par five….about 490 yards. It had trees on the right and out of bounds on the left. A bunker was on the right about halfway down. Each had good drives….Alex was to the right but trees did not impede his second shot. Emmett's drive left his ball slightly to the left of the center of the fairway, nearly as far as Alex's shot. Their second shots avoided the bunker and left them about ninety yards from the green. Alex hit an excellent approach, leaving him with only a ten foot putt. Emmett's was also close but on the other side of the pin leaving him with an uphill sharply breaking putt of about thirteen feet. Alex drained his putt….Emmett's was very close but didn't break as much as he had hoped.

"Do you know what Einstein described as the Eighth Wonder of the World?" Emmett asked Alex.

"E=MC Squared." Alex replied.

" 'Compound Interest' is what Einstein spoke of." Emmett stated.

"Have you taken advantage of our company's 401(k) Roth option?"

Emmett asked.

"Not really." Alex answered. "Because my income is reasonably good, my accountant suggested that I maximize my pre-tax contribution."

"Considering the long term growth, that recommendation may be short sighted." Emmett stated.

"How is that?" Alex queried.

"Well if you contribute $ 250,000 into your 401(k) over the next thirty years and you are in an average tax bracket of 20% you have saved $ 50,000 in taxes. With even modest returns, those contributions will grow to over $ 800,000 in thirty years and continue to grow in retirement. In another ten or twelve years it will be over 1.6 million. Do you want to save the tax on the $250,000 or the 1.6 million?" Emmett asked.

"I guess compound interest is the Eighth Wonder of the World." Alex stated.

Nine was another par four with only modest hazards.....water to the right and out of bounds on the left. Both men hit their drives well and fairly straight. Emmett's was slightly shorter and nearer the center of the fairway....his second shot landed to the left of the green about forty yards from the pin.

Alex's second shot went to the right of the green leaving him an uphill approach from under some trees. Emmett chipped onto the green leaving him about an eighteen foot putt. Alex had to keep his chip low because of the tree hanging over his lie. His shot ran to the left edge of the green leaving him twenty feet from the pin. Both men two putted.

"How did you learn so much about finance and retirement?" Alex asked.

"I learned most of it from the advisor we changed to a few years ago as we got closer to retirement. There are a few things I learned on my own. I have always been a student of history. Did you know that Roman soldiers near the time of Christ were given 12 years of wages in a lump sum and six acres of land as a retirement pension after 20-25 years of service ?" Emmett asked.

"I had no idea that retirement plans had been around that long."

Alex answered.

"Some forty or fifty years ago if an employee had any kind of retirement plan where he worked, it was likely a pension. Some companies, like Studebaker, were unable to fund their retired employees' pensions adequately. When the government stepped in to protect employees, new regulations made it very difficult for businesses to offer pensions, hence the rise of 401(k)s, which leave all the responsibility for retirement with the employee." Emmett digressed.

Emmett and Alex got a refreshment from the clubhouse prior to walking out to their cart which was parked near the tee for the tenth hole. It was warmer than when they started....the beverage that each of them drank provided some needed hydration.

The tenth hole stretches to the west, a view of the Colorado mountains lies behind the green in the distance on this straight 410 yard par four. A miss-hit to the left will put your tee shot in water.....tall mature trees along the right don't present a huge problem unless your tee shot ends up right behind one, which is where Alex's drive landed. Emmett's shorter drive was slightly to the left of the center of the fairway.

Alex used an iron to get his ball back into play.....a little closer to the green than he was behind the tree.

Emmett hit his second shot a little to the right and short of the green by about 30 yards. Alex's third shot landed very near Emmett's.

Both chipped onto the green and two putted.

"Alex, I've been talking about me and retirement the whole time we've been out here. How are you and Kathy doing?"

"We are doing fine. We've been in our new home for about a year and plan to start a family very soon. She likes her work as a nurse and when we have children she can work some part time shifts at the hospital where some other nurses with families are doing the same.

We have some long range plans of getting a place in the mountains, since we both love to ski, bike and enjoy the outdoors. " Alex explained.

"It sounds like you and Kathy have done some planning of your own."

Emmett commented.

"That's true, Emmett, since we have fairly good income, we would like that to be working for us both for the present and the future. I have an older brother and although he is very talented, he never seems to get ahead financially. He spends money foolishly and has often asked our parents for help."

"You and Kathy sound like you are both on a much sounder footing than he is." Emmett said.

"We think so....and thanks for the compliment. Kathy and I try to do what's right." Alex added.

The eleventh hole was a 510 yard par five with a bunker on the left of the fairway about one third of the way to the green, out of bounds on the right and that same creek about ninety yards in front of the green.

Each hit drives just to the right of the bunker....Alex's lying just slightly farther ahead. Alex hit a fairway wood longer than he anticipated and ended up in the creek. Emmett's second shot left him about 150 yards from the pin and sixty yards in front of the creek. Alex took a penalty stroke and hit from in front of the creek landing his shot near the middle of the green leaving him a fifteen foot putt. Emmett hit a very good iron shot and landed near the front of the green leaving him a long putt of about 25 feet. Alex missed his putt leaving him with a bogie. Emmett two putted for his par.

"Emmett, when you and Jane met with your new advisor, what was that like? Was he a pushy sales guy?" Alex asked.

"No and No. She was not pushy and not a guy. She has many years of experience in financial services, a very competent staff and for the last ten years has specialized in retirement planning. She does educational meetings at churches, service clubs, libraries and recreation centers in and around the Denver area. We met her at one of those events." Emmett answered.

The twelve hole was a 400 yard par four with a dog leg to the right. A bunker and out of bounds were on the left...trees on the right. They each hit their drives slightly to the right but in the fairway....This time Emmett's drive went slightly further. Alex cut the corner and got in a little trouble as his second shot landed behind some trees to the right of the green. Emmett's shot was short but left him an easy approach from 20 yards in front of the green. Alex's approach ran past the green to the right on the fringe. Emmett chipped onto the green leaving him with an eighteen foot putt. Each used two more strokes to finish the hole.

"So did your advisor provide you with a plan based on what most other people are doing?"

"Right from our first meeting she made it clear that if we were uncomfortable working with her we could exit the process....or if she felt she would be unable to help us she would let us know. She didn't plug our information into a computer to create a plan.....instead, Lori, our advisor, provided assistance so that we were able to create our own plan.

She asked a lot of questions over several meetings in her office before she came up with some solutions based on our goals and unique situation." Emmett Explained.

Thirteen was a par three.....not a long hole but over water, about one hundred seventy yards to the pin.... one hundred twenty yards to clear the water. Both Emmett and Alex made it over the water. Alex may have used too much club as his shot went past the green and remained on the grassy mound behind it.

Alex's shot landed to the right on the apron about pin high, just missing a sand trap which was on the right of the green. He was left with an uphill putt (or chip) breaking to the right.... about 25 feet from the pin. Alex lifted his chip shot high and fortunately it did not roll too far down the green, leaving him with a twelve foot putt. Emmett used his putter and nearly drained his long putt as it rolled five feet past the pin.

Alex made his long putt... Emmett made his short one and they each pared the hole.

"How can you and Jane be sure that your plan will work?" Alex asked

"When Lori helped us create our plan, she included a lot of flexibility. She showed us how we could divide our assets into three buckets....one for bank money for an emergency fund with about six months of our regular expenses. The second bucket is for guaranteed income from various sources.

This is the most important because it represents the money we will need to live on well into the future. The last bucket is money in the market which is liquid but also at moderate risk.

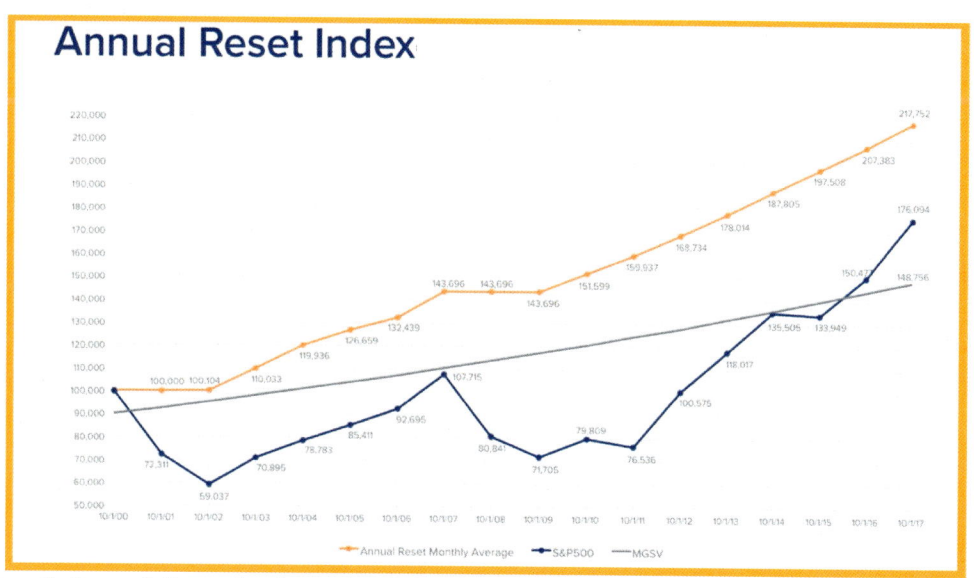

Lori explained that although there is risk, those assets are tactically managed. That means that our level of risk is mitigated based on our comfort level and risk tolerance." Emmett Explained.

Fourteen was another par four....about 410 yards... with a bunker on the right and a gulley full of weeds (and possibly rattlesnakes) about 70 yards short of the green. The gulley crossed the entire fairway.

Emmett's drive went slightly to the right, short of the bunker. Alex's was longer and to the left. On his second shot Emmett was slightly short of the green and to the right, easily clearing the gulley. Alex shanked his iron shot. It scooted along the ground rolling into the gulley. He was able to find his ball....and two other Titleists.

Although his ball was in the gulley, it was playable. He blasted out of the weeds, landing on the front of the green. Emmett chipped onto the green, his shot left him even closer to the pin. He drained his putt....Alex two putted.

Fifteen was a straightaway par five....about 500 yards with water on the right about halfway down. The Left was out of bounds, but the fairway was wide. Bunkers were on the left, extending nearly to the middle of the fairway. Both Alex and Emmett hit shots near the center of the fairway....Alex's went about ten yards further. Alex sliced his second shot into the water, Emmett's was only slightly to the right, landing about one hundred yards from the green. Alex took his penalty stroke and on his next shot landed about seventy yards short of the green to the left. On their next shots, both reached the green with Alex's shot landing about ten feet from the pin. Alex made the putt....Emmett two putted, getting his par.

"I've really enjoyed hearing about the process you and Jane went through as you planned your retirement. You said your old advisor had done ok. Did you have any concerns that your money might have done better had you stayed with him?"

"Good question, Alex. Before Jane and I made the change, we met with one other advisor before we met Lori.

He seemed like a nice guy but didn't focus on what Jane and felt was most important. When we met Lori, one thing she did was provide us with a portfolio analysis of our existing holdings. Although our old advisor had helped us grow our money, the analysis showed us the level of risk we would be carrying into retirement, which was greater than either of us wanted.

The analysis also showed the performance of our underlying investments and how that compared to other alternatives. It also revealed fees we were paying, not only management fees but also some of the underlying fees associated with the mutual funds he had placed us in. Once we had seen this information, our decision was easy." Emmett explained.

Sixteen was a par three with an elevated green, making approaches somewhat difficult. Sand traps were on the left of the green, mature trees on the right. It was about 165 yards. Emmett's shot left him a little short but right in front of the green about ten yards from the edge. Pin placement was near the middle right. Alex reached the green near the back left, leaving himself a thirty foot putt.

Emmett executed an excellent chip shot leaving him only five feet from the hole. Alex's putt had a break to the right making it long and tricky.

He had a good line but not enough juice…..leaving the putt four feet short. Both pared the hole.

Seventeen was a dog leg left and slightly uphill, about a 415 yard par four. Younger trees were on the left in the rough. On the right between fairways were tall mature trees. The rough on both sides was long. One bunker provided a hazard on the right about halfway down the fairway.

Alex hit a good drive but it went to the right and landed in the bunker… but he was left with a good lie. Emmett hit the same direction but his drive landed just short of the bunker.

Alex hit a clean shot out of the bunker landing pin high just to the right of the long green. Emmett hit a good second shot which landed on the front of the long green. The pin placement was in the back and the green was gently sloping uphill and to the right. Emmett was left with at least a thirty foot putt.

Alex chipped onto the green, ending up only seven feet from the pin. Emmett's long putt was only slightly off line and rolled four feet past the pin. Both men made their putts and pared this hole also.

"It sounds like you and Jane are financially secure, but how do you both plan to spend your time, now that you will have so much of it?" Alex asked. "

"Both Jane and I are active in our church which involves some volunteering. That may also involve some short term mission trips to help less fortunate believers in other countries.

Our son lives in Seattle so we plan to travel there a few times each year so that we can spoil our grandkids. Also Jane has some family who live in the Midwest so we will be making a few trips there also. In addition we both have some more ambitious travel plans. Jane has always wanted to go to New Zealand. She does weaving and that country is famous for its wool and fabric arts inert general. I would love to visit Ireland one spring. I have family roots there and I believe it would be a great experience to see where my ancestors lived." Emmett explained.

"Won't that kind of extravagant travel be expensive?" Alex asked.

"Jane and I created an LLC called "EJ International." After each trip we will be writing a blog about the experience and posting pictures that will be available for sale. The sale of the pictures and the advertisers who are attracted to the blog will generate some income, AND as long as we are genuinely attempting to generate income, the travel expenses are, for the most part, tax deductible." Emmett explained.

Eighteen was a short (370 yards) par four with water directly in front of the tee and extending about one hundred and thirty yards. Tall trees on both sides presented the only other hazards. Unlike the rest of the round, Emmett shanked his drive and hit one in the water. He laughed and pointed out that this was his only poor drive all day and it had to happen on a water hole. He hit again and easily cleared the water but was lying three with his penalty stroke. Alex hit a good drive but slightly to the right between some tall trees. Both men reached the green on their second shots and two putted to finish the round.

"Emmett, it sounds like you and Jane have really thought this through, your retirement and all. What recourse do you have if things don't go according to your plan?" Alex asked.

"Another good question, Alex. Our advisor, Lori, meets with us regularly to see if any of our circumstances have changed. Our plan is very flexible and would easily allow an increase in our income if we felt it necessary. Working with Lori is an ongoing process rather than a series of one or two events." Emmett explained.

"I really enjoyed this round of Golf with you Emmett…and I would like Lori's contact information." Alex said as they headed to clubhouse to add up their scores and enjoy a refreshing beverage.

"Sure." Emmett Replied.

Emmett

Alex

L to R...Emmett, Golfer nearby (Todd), Alex, Golfer (Brian), playing with Golfer nearby (Todd).

THE END

Epilogue - Post Retirement Planning

As an American and a Christian I believe that we are truly blessed. Someone who lives in the United States, who has very few assets, is still likely to have a standard of living far higher than most of the rest of the world. The economic advantages we enjoy along with the assets we have accumulated permit us to be a beacon of hope for many of the less fortunate, both here in the United States and in the rest of the world.

In working with retirees and those preparing for retirement, I've learned that some people have a sense of fulfillment and joy that is a bi-product of their giving back to others who are less fortunate. That may be veterans, the disabled or seniors who need a caregiver but can't afford one. For each one of us who enjoys the fruits of our years of labor, there are others who need help. It may not be financial, it may be just for them to know that someone cares.

I believe God has a purpose for each one of us. How we spend our time and resources in retirement has to go beyond finding a new hobby or completing a bucket list. The happiest retirees I've met are not the ones with the highest net worth......instead they are those who have listened to His voice and found purpose in their lives in doing His work.
- Al Smith

ACKNOWLEDGEMENT

A special thanks for time and creative edit to...

Sarah E. Herbert owner of BUNIWORX

sarah@buniworx.com
www.buniworx.com

&

Autumn Nelson of GOLDEN EAGLE FINANCIAL
autumn@goldeneaglefinancialltd.com
www.goldeneaglefinancialltd.com

GOLDEN EAGLE FINANCIAL LTD.

ABOUT THE AUTHOR

Al Smith

Al lives in Littleton and has been working with people in financial areas for over thirty years. He has three children and six grandchildren. He enjoys skiing, hiking, cycling and living in Colorado where these activities thrive.

He is an elder in his church, Redemption Hills, where he and other family members attend. His financial education includes being a Chartered Life Underwriter, a Chartered Financial Consultant and a Certified Financial Educator.

In addition to working with clients at his local office, Al speaks to service clubs, recreation centers and retirement communities about "Memory Improvement" and "Finding Your Purpose in Retirement." Although his work is financial in nature, Al feels that helping people in these other areas as they approach retirement is extremely important. Al discusses these topics further on his radio show 'Retirement Unpacked' where you can hear him live every Wednesday at 2:00pm on KLZ 560AM.

Al believes that we can continue to grow, learn and contribute regardless of our age. Al is a fiduciary.

Made in the USA
Columbia, SC
21 August 2022